RAISE UP
THE LOW
BRING DOWN
THE MIGHTY

ASHER HOYLES
PERFORMANCE POETRY

INCLUDES CDs

HANSIB

First published in Great Britain by Hansib Publications in 2018

Hansib Publications Limited
P.O. Box 226, Hertford, SG14 3WY, UK

info@hansibpublications.com
www.hansibpublications.com

ISBN 978-1-910553-92-3

A CIP catalogue record for this book
is available from the British Library

Design & Production by Hansib Publications Ltd
Printed in Great Britain

DEDICATION

To Martin and Rosa with all my love

ACKNOWLEDGEMENTS

I would like to thank all the following for their great help and inspiration in producing this book: Arif, Kash & Shareef Ali, Jean 'Binta' Breeze, Anna Maria & Olly Brill, Clean Break staff & students, Gary Douglas, Paula Edwards, Kat Francois, Zita Holbourne, Martin & Rosa Hoyles, Annwen Johnson, Sara La Rosa and family, Lucienne Latour, Silvana Lennon, Prince Jacob Louear and family, Paul Lyalls, Mica McKenzie, Gary Mclaren, Sam McNeil, Michael Maraise, NewVic staff & students, Paddy from Survivors, Brandon Rackal & family, Michael Rosen, Marrik Shearer, Juley Smith, Cara & Carina Smithen, Myra & Vincent Smithen, Duncan Thornley, David & Judith Wood, Benjamin Zephaniah.

CONTENTS

Youth

Racism and Sexism

Nature

History and Politics

Happiness

INTRODUCTION

Asher Hoyles, whose mother comes from Nevis in the West Indies, was born in Leeds on 12 December 1966. She was brought up in Chapeltown and had a strict childhood. At a very early age she had responsibilities around the house, such as cooking and cleaning, which were sometimes carried out reluctantly because she longed to be playing outside.

In primary school she realised she had the ability to tell stories and liked writing them too. She still remembers a poem which she wrote for a competition:

> Mr Lawford is a very funny man
> He's got long legs and he loves to dance
> But if you get him in a very bad mood
> You better not come to school
> He's got a stick as big as this
> He's tried it on me
> He'll try it on you
> So if I were you
> I'd just stay cool!

Asher won some sweets for this poem, but writing poetry was not really encouraged. She also liked listening to stories and particularly remembers a teacher, called Mr Nelson, reading *Catweazle*, doing all the characters in their different voices. She enjoyed going swimming and played the violin until it was stolen from the school. At secondary school she liked drama and remembers being in *A Midsummer Night's Dream* and Brecht's *Caucasian Chalk Circle*, produced by her art teacher David Wood.

On the whole, however, she did not like school subjects and was lacking in self-confidence. She later wrote a poem about school called 'Ting a Ling' challenging the view that your schooldays are the best days of your life:

> I remember dat lie
> Wid forty children in de class
> Routine task
> Teacher a bawl
> How ungrateful we are
> Me hatred of maths
> Being bottom of the class
> Answering back
> Getting a slap.

The first section of the book, Childhood and Culture, reflects this period in her life.

On Saturdays Asher went with her mother to the Seventh Day Adventist church where Sister Baker often used to ask her to recite poems and passages from the bible: 'I had to learn them by heart. I knew people liked to hear me, so there must have been something about my voice that people approved of. I remember going up there and my mum sitting there looking proud. It was all about being the best that you can. I learnt standards. You had to do it well. It was the same with cooking. You had to make sure you did things to the best of your ability.'

Another experience of performing came about when Asher was fourteen: 'Chatting lyrics on the mic in Chapeltown was my earliest experience of poetry, though we never called it that. The fact of being a woman was important too, and getting respect from the male MCs.'

She also received some informal education: 'Educationally we weren't brought up to understand anything about our history or background. Rastaman was coming forward with a new perspective on things that made me inquisitive. What was this place called Africa? What's this thing about roots? I was being told I belonged somewhere and that felt really good, even though I didn't know where to find Africa on a map! That was positive. I was growing up where people were saying "Go back to your own country!" Where? I was born here! It was all very confusing and all I used to say was "It's not fair!"'

> When I was a youth and living in Yorkshire
> I never knew a thing about my African culture
> The first time I came across the term retention
> I really did believe it was a physical condition
> It was only when I listened to the music of the rasta
> And I heard in the lyrics we were going back to Africa.
> ('Retention Attention')

At the age of fifteen Asher left Leeds for London (see the section on Leaving Home), but it was not till some years later when she went to university that she started writing poetry: 'I always had difficulty writing and at university I discovered I was dyslexic. Poetry became important to me as a way of expressing things in the way that I wanted to. I wanted to stamp my own voice on things. I'd previously written songs for bands I had been in. Then I started to show my friend Michael some of my poems and he gave me a lot of encouragement. I didn't really write the poems, but composed them in my head and out loud. When they were finished, then I wrote them down.'

The poetry was very therapeutic: 'I always wanted to be committed to something and strangely being dyslexic led to an interest in writing poetry to express how I was feeling. I was very tense at that time and writing poetry got rid of a lot of frustrations. At last I was beginning to find my own voice and I was becoming more politically aware. I realised I had so much to say.'

The first poem she wrote was called 'Hot Water in Your Place', about responsibilities in the home:

> When I was a child
> My mother used to have a golden rule
> She used to say
> Always have hot water in your place
> Not just for cooking
> But for your emergencies.

Her first performance was at Bunjie's in Charing Cross Road: 'It was the most nerve-wracking experience, hands sweating, very shaky and nervous, scared out of my wits. My next venue was Chat's Palace in Hackney, with a mainly black audience. I was very frightened, but when people came up afterwards and asked me questions about my poetry, it was very encouraging. It makes you want to do more.'

Since then she has performed at many venues, including the Hay-on-Wye festival, the Institute of Contemporary Arts, Glastonbury, Survivors' Poetry, Stratford Theatre Royal and

bunjies in exile
146 charing cross road
nearest tube tottenham court road

Monday January 3rd

PETER CADLE
CAROLINE DAVID

Monday January 10th

ALAN TATE
ASHER HOYLES

Monday January 17th

JUDITH SILVER
NYKI BLATCHLEY

Monday January 3rd

JON BRINDLEY
SIMON SELIGMAN

8:30pm start
Prices: £3.50, £2.50 concessions, £1.50 floorspots

MC JOHN PEACOCK
0171-928 4790
07932 642580

N.A.M
New Acoustic Movement

Performance Poetry by Asher Hoyles

on the street at the Stoke Newington summer festival. She has been to schools and colleges, libraries and community centres, pubs and clubs, and led poetry workshops at Maidstone Men's Prison and Rayleigh Women's Prison. Her poems have also been displayed on London buses. In October 2001 she was proud to share a platform in Camden with John la Rose (New Beacon) and Jessica Huntley (Bogle-L'Ouverture), the first black publishers in Britain, as she performed her poems in celebration of black history month. In February 2009 Asher performed her poem 'The Talking Book' in Westminster Abbey (St Margaret's Church) at the dedication of the memorial plaque to the black abolitionist Olaudah Equiano.

Asher sees performance poetry as an 'opportunity to use every part of my body to express my experiences as a black woman. The poetry is lifted off the page and moves around. It moves with your body, with expression. There'll be times when I'm moving my hips, tapping my feet, nodding my head, moving my arms around. I find reading some poetry very difficult and it takes the pleasure away, but performing poetry can help you understand it more easily (see Performance Poetry and the Oral Tradition). You're very vulnerable, however, as a performance poet. You're there with your own material that you've written yourself. It's not acting, a play, a production, where you're pretending to be something you're not. It's a very responsible position. I'm a nervous person who's learnt to be courageous!'

As regards publishing, Asher used to say: 'People have asked me if they can buy my book and I have to say that I have no book yet, but if you want a particular poem I will send you a copy. If I was ever to publish, I would like people to hear the poems as well, so they can understand them better, so they can hear the rhythm, whether it's a rap or a song or a chat.'

Her favourite poets are Benjamin Zephaniah, Linton Kwesi Johnson and Jean 'Binta' Breeze, because their poetry is 'accessible and reminds me of reggae'. Linton Kwesi Johnson was speaking for the younger generation who were suffering from such low expectations in school. While he was commenting on the Brixton riots, Asher saw parts of Chapeltown burnt down.

She likes Maya Angelou too, because she presents herself confidently as a big woman and is a positive role model. In

Jean 'Binta' Breeze   **Maya Angelou (1928-2014)**

'Phenomenal Woman', for example, she writes of herself
as a strong black woman:

> Pretty women wonder where my secret lies.
> I'm not cute or built to suit a fashion model's size
> But when I start to tell them,
> They think I'm telling lies.
> I say,
> It's in the reach of my arms,
> The span of my hips,
> The stride of my step,
> The curl of my lips.
> I'm a woman
> Phenomenally.
> Phenomenal woman,
> That's me.

One of Asher's favourite poems is Shelley's 'Mask of Anarchy', about the massacre of demonstrators at Peterloo, Manchester, in 1819, which begins:

As I lay asleep in Italy
There came a voice from over the Sea,
And with great power it forth led me
To walk in the visions of Poesy.

She likes the poem because it talks about 'oppression and exploitation, but also, as Bob Marley says, about a small axe cutting down a big tree', as the chorus goes:

Rise like Lions after slumber
In unvanquishable number,
Shake your chains to earth like dew
Which in sleep had fallen on you -
Ye are many - they are few.

Some of the main themes of her own poetry are racism, exploitation in the work-place, history and women's rights. 'The Rebellious One', for example, begins:

**Percy Bysshe Shelley
(1792-1822)**

I am Africa steeped in sun
I am where the story begun
For I am the rebellious one
Working the land
And praying for freedom.

As for writing her poems: 'The first line is very important and sometimes takes a long time to come. But the time will come when the poem arrives, either in spurts or piece by piece by piece till eventually it's there. A poem can come to me anywhere: on the street, at my desk, washing the dishes, doing housework. I do enjoy composing poetry.'

She believes more could be done in schools to encourage a love of poetry: 'You've got to be able to identify with it in some way. For some people it's just too complicated. And it's not always taught enthusiastically. It would help to have more poets in schools and get students to write their own poetry about whatever they want. They have to see the connection between what Shakespeare and Shelley were writing about and their own situation now. I wasn't allowed to study Shakespeare, but having seen several of his plays, including *King Lear* with Robert Stephens, I can now quote from the play:

THE VOICE

WHERE THERE'S LIFE THERE'S HOPE

Clean Break performance poetry booklet 2012

The weight of this sad time we must obey;
Speak what we feel, not what we ought to say.
The oldest hath borne most: we that are young,
Shall never see so much, nor live so long.

Asher has run regular poetry workshop sessions with students at Clean Break Theatre Company in Kentish Town and her constant advice is: 'Read as much as possible and listen to tapes of poetry. Go out and listen to performance poets. Have some faith in you own ability and in your own experience. It might not be the best poem ever written, but it will be a start!'

After finishing her degree in Education and Communication Studies at the University of East London, Asher went to work at NewVic Sixth Form College in Plaistow, East London, where she is now a Learning Support Practitioner in the Special Needs Department. She has been there for over twenty years and during that time has qualified as a teacher and gained a postgraduate certificate in Dyslexia from University College London.

This book is the first which Asher has written on her own, but she is also the co-author, with her husband of *Remember Me: Achievements of Mixed-Race People, Past & Present* (1999), *Moving Voices: Black Performance Poetry* (2002), *Dyslexia from a Cultural Perspective* (2007) and *Caribbean Publishing in Britain: A Tribute to Arif Ali* (2011)

(Adapted from *Moving Voices*, Hansib 2002)

CHILDHOOD AND CULTURE

CHAPELTOWN

Chapeltown is where me come from
Where me use to sport me Afro hair
An put on me flares
Where Blacker's sound
Had the sharpest lyrics around
An reggae music would fill up Chapeltown's air

When summer days could be spent playing champ
Or watching a group of girls cussing their man
Or watching a group of boys a argue
About which one a them is lyric bantan

**Angela Davis with
an afro, 1971**

An in the distance you could hear
Somebody's mum
Come in an give me a hand
You don't have no ambition
Deh pan de street so long

Dem de kinda tings use to gi' me joke
An mek me laugh
For a Chapeltown is where me come from

Yes there was poverty
But there was a sense of community
The older generation passed on their traditions
They give we rice an peas
Sweet potato an yam
To mek we strong
An we all did look forward to de carnival
An wedder we like it or not
We get we dose of religion

For many a dem did tink
We need some spiritual inspiration
As a form of protection
For dem did know from time
About police corruption

An although we did understan dem intention
The second generation had their objections
Especially with high unemployment
A poor standard of education
An continually treated
Like second-class citizens

An instead of de media speak out
About the pressure we under
Dem come in instead wid dem propaganda

They say it is only a working-class area
Full a drug dealers
Where black people are causing terror
Where prostitution is rife
Where Jack the Ripper stole some lives

They never did say
It was the place
Where many West Indians came
To work hard to survive
Some turned a blind eye
To tings dat wasn't right
In order for dem and dem children
Fe live a little life

That despite the poverty
And the exposed dishonesty
Chapeltown could still
Celebrate summer times
And life.

DARE TO DREAM THE DREAM

There once was a woman
Who dared to dream the dream
There she goes, rocking to an fro
On the boat that would bring her to England

She wash
She cook
She clean
She iron
She standing by she children an she man

An every mickle must make a muckle in her hand
As she scrapes togedda to buy de piece a yam
She remembers how it used to grow in abundance
In her home land

She coulda never buy nuttin expensive
But with a skill create something out of nothing
If only to show her children
How to make the most of a little thing

The dream she had then had faded
Like a bubble disappearing from her hand
But she wants a better future for her children
And she also wants to reach the promised land.

SS *Empire Windrush* arriving at Tilbury, 22 June 1948, with around 500 passengers from the Caribbean

---

THE FAMILY CLASSROOM

Girl, you got to learn to tink for yourself
Spin and turn your hand
You're not going to reach the party on time
And late to reach inside God's house

Learn to do the small things
And the big things will come after
And while you living underneath my roof
You're not to talk back to you mudda

Your father put the bread on the table
A beg all you have some manners
You don't see how are you does mek me bex
When me see you don't have no conscience

But am not going to live for ever
And who can't hear must feel
Better dat you come inside and pick up a book
An keep your tail part off de street

For de teacher say you get nought out a ten
Dat no sound too good to me
Nought out a ten
Nought out a ten
You not even going to get to sweep de streets

An no look in a me face
When I'm not talking to you
You need to learn to mind your business
You had de right in your hand
An you lose it now
By the way you went about it

You can hide from a tief
Yes hide from a tief
But what you going to do wid de liar
Better dat you get yourself baptised
An follow de good example of your sista

For de other day I nearly shot you a box
When me hear how you did talk to the minister
When him ask you if you want to get baptised
And you tell him say you don't want to waste de water!

HAIR

There was Afro
And cane row
Single plaits too
Ring combs for bunches
In ones and in twos
And for all de hair styles
Dat deh pan display
A never did learn
How to comb my hair

A run to me mumma
'Mumma, please comb my hair.'
'No, child, de combing and de plaiting
Give me fingers dem pain.'
Send me to me sister
An me sister complain
'You's me little sister
But you really is a pain.
Why you don't learn
Learn to comb your hair?'

Me bark after her
And say, 'You don't care!'
She kiss her teeth
And leave me hair same way

So me tek up de comb
Me tek up de grease
I garn to auntie Christine
For she lives in our street
She comes from Nevis

She strict but she sweet
And she can plait my hair so very very neat
In all de latest hair styles
Me does see out a street

So me brace up meself to ask her to do it
Because me timing wasn't good
So hear how she drop it

'Come in
Sit down
How is dad and mum?
You come to comb your hair
And is now you just a come?
What happen to de hair style
A did give you last week?
So much tings to do
Lawd have his mercy!'

Still she cussing
And she parting
She cussing
And she plaiting
She say me muss keep me hand out a me head
Because me hair is not growing

And on the surface me look sorry
But inside me heart me smiling
For she doing de pineapple style me like
Me going to look good in school dis morning

Amongst the Afro
The cane row
The single plaits too
Ring combs for bunches
In ones and in twos
And am not going to look silly
And am not going to feel shame
And maybe one day
I'll learn to comb my hair!

TING A LING

Ting a ling a ling
School bell ring
Put on your uniform
And get in a de swing
And don't waste time
Be on time
Remember your school days
Are the best days of your life

I remember dat lie
As I walked reluctantly to school
Wid me heart full a dread
Wondering which bully a go try bus in my head
Tek me money from me pocket
Rip up me jacket
Stick me head down the toilet
I remember it well

Ting a ling a ling…

I remember dat lie
Wid forty children in the class
Routine task
Teacher a bawl how ungrateful we are
Me hatred of maths
Being bottom of the class
Answering back
Getting a slap

Ting a ling a ling…

I remember dat lie
In me skimpy gym clothes
In de freezing cold
Wid me puppy fat a flap
Wid boys by the railings making wise cracks
Wid wise teachers in coats and scarves
Coffee in hand
While others tried to control the open rebellion

Ting a ling a ling
Bell stop ring
And now I'm only reminiscing
But as I reflect upon much time gone by
I still find myself
Still find myself remembering, ring, ring, ring
Remembering.

RICE NOT SPICE

'Sophie! buy a bag a rice
Quarter pound a onion
Tek de money from me purse
Run go and come
Buy de half a dozen egg
An de one fresh bun
Tek de money from me purse
Run go and come
Buy de margarine me like
You know de one dat I mean
De one dat I does use to do me baking
Nobodda mek your father a fine you a chat pan de street
Grab de shopping bag an go deh quick.'

An a so Sophie left in a maximum speed
An when she know her mamma couldn't see
De running turn into strolling
De strolling turn into stopping
De stopping turn into talking
An she no remember de shopping
Until it start to darken
An de urgency set back een
An then she run
An de first shop she come to
She went in an she buy
One bag a spice
Half a dozen egg
A bottle a cooking oil
An de last buns pan top de man shelf
An then she run an she run
Ca she want reach home before her farder come

An just as she reach de door
It open an her mamma say
'What time you call dis?
A dis you mean by quick
Bring de shopping in come gimme.'
An a so she start check it
An when she see what Sophie bring
She put down one cussing:
'It's really coming to something
When you can't send your chile shopping
A ask you for rice
She bring back spice
Me no see no onion
Or margarine in a my eye sight
An me know dis was de lass buns
From top de man shelf
You know how me know
Ca it hard is a shame
An when de ting hard
You know dat it stale
Tek dat look up off a your face
Ca na you done spen off me change
Me no know nothing about vex
Me know nothing about shame
Put de tings back in de bag
An tek dem back!'

BACK TO CARIBBEAN BASICS

You can pronounce your words eloquently
Make every syllable sound fresh and clean
Wear a suit so crisp
With a seam so sharp
You really could trip over it
You could have a house stretching over acres of land
And money in the bank
But you won't get on with any West Indian you meet
If you don't have a ting call manners.

HOT WATER IN YOUR PLACE

When I was a child
My mother used to have a golden rule
She used to say
Always have hot water in your place
Not just for cooking
But for your emergencies

When I was a child
My father had his golden rules
Sweep down the stairs
Clean out the television room
And when you're done
Go find a book
It is important for a child to find something to do

You see when I was a child
Life wasn't just about play
Life was about taking on your responsibilities
I never used to like it
And me face used to long
And me mudda used to say
You see that girl
She lazy lazy bad

It is only now that I am older
And I get to understan
What it tek
To be a big woman
For me get to learn
And see for meself
The respec you can get
When people can see you doing tings for yourself

So my advice to man, woman or child
Always have hot water in your place
Not just for cooking
But for your emergencies.

LEAVING HOME

ALTERNATIVE ACCOMMODATION

Two young girls in a hostel disco
Fresh from leaving home
One with a pint of cider
The other with a rum and coke

The punk rock beat is sounding
To them it sounds astonishing
Standing in their red gold and green
Dem a wait to hear the reggae stylee

For that style is more familiar
For them a hole them pose
Are they badass girls in a de area
Or strangers far from home

Can't get no reggae stylee tonight
But we can catch a little ska
Start to move we hips a little
Then the trouble starts

A man dat look about five foot eight
Body like him addicted to weights
Grab de drink out a my fren hand
An blam we coolness garn

As two young girls start to mek dem demands
To fine out what a gwan
De man start to laugh
And say we must tek up we tings
From out of dem corridor
For you two girls can't stay in a dis hostel no more

Aswad, London 1984

An a so we get mad
An start to get on bad
An jump up pon top de man
An tump an a slap
An a cuss plenty bad word
An a tell dem say you can't
Treat we so jus ca we black

Then the music stop
So we just barge out a dem disco
An knock down tings along de way
An a tell dem in no uncertain terms
You really mek a mistake
If you feel that you can treat we any kinda way

When we went into the corridor
Me buck up pon de manager
Him looking kinda shame
Me just look him in him face
An say you better start to explain

Well im tell me dis
Im tell me dat
But inna my ears
It sounds like crap
An after very little negotiation
An plenty incrimination
Me just tell him say you better
Fine we some alternative accommodation

Dem tek up we tings
Fling we tings we included
In the back of the van
Driving the van
Like how you does see police driving criminals
To the next hostel

When we reach dem just fling out we tings we included
    an garn
When we went into reception
Me know the woman know the situation
So me just ask she for a key
You know what the feisty woman have the cheek to ask
    me
If me have any money

She must have see say me eyes a fill up red
An me mouth just push out
For she give me de key
She know me tired and me vex
An me just want to rest

When we wake up in de mornin
We in a room full a man
We do all within we power
To stifle we laugh

But a so we get we first lesson
About de rugged side of London
And how it is not always glamorous
To say you are independent.

THE LONDON UNDERGROUND

There is something quite peculiar
About the London Underground
It is not as straight forward
As just getting us around

It's not even de way we cram up
Inside de tube like sardines in a can
Or de way some people holding on to the seat
Dem holding on to the seat
Like dem life is dependent upon it

No it's not dat

It is de way some a we surrender
To the hidden agenda
The code of silence while important business types
And the like read their newspapers

Don't you see the way they flick dem
Wid frustration when somebody a talk
And if you have de audacity to open a packet of crisps
Why dem look you in you face like you should be
        arrested

Those of you who read the papers
Like the Times and Independent
Yes you know who you are
Invading me bit a space
Shaking de newspaper
All up inna me face

It is only brave people and tourist
Come on de tube and laugh
For they know these newspaper readers
Don't have the authority to throw dem off

You see
Laughing to them is like creating a disturbance
Invading their privacy
Breaking their code of silence
But nothing annoys the newspaper reader more
Than being sat next to the not-so-personal stereo

There's something quite peculiar
About the London Underground
If you are ever on there
Have a look around.

SWEET SIXTEEN

Caught within the spell of a London hotel
I was sweet sixteen
And apart from sharing a room with six
Vi was trying to convince me that she was in fact a witch
She was around forty
Her hair a murky orange
Make-up badly placed upon her face
Wearing a negligee that had seen better days
She spoke of how she'd lived here for years

Caught, caught within the spell of a London hotel
I was sweet sixteen
And apart from sharing a room with six
There was Bill he was a schizophrenic
He would tear off his clothes
Go running up and down the corridors
Shouting and screaming obscenities
But when he wasn't doing that
He was rather friendly
He would carry a suit-case, not full of clothes
But cutlery and other necessities
You could always stop Bill
For a friendly chat
For sugar tea or coffee

Caught, caught within the spell of a London hotel
I was sweet sixteen
And apart from sharing a room with six
There was the tragedy of Nicki
She had run away from home
To have a life of her own

From Slough she had come to the big city
And what struck me about Nicki
She was pretty
She could have been a model
Or someone famous you see off the telly
Instead she just cried herself to sleep
Too deep in the drug scene
It wasn't long before what was a comfort to her
Was getting speed or heroin

Caught, caught within the spell of a London hotel
I was sweet sixteen
And although I'm trying to be objective
That phenomenon included me
Sweet sixteen.

BACK IN TIME

I'm going back in time
To the days of Gipton Avenue
When playing at weddings
Was something you did for a laugh
When you didn't mind too much
If a little girl played the part of the man
Back to the days when your commitment to stay faithful
    and true
Only lasted until the game was through

Back to the days when 1996
Was as far away as the moon
As far away removed as the words 'I do'

Back to the days of being able to stay out late
The luscious smell of sugar cakes
And wondering why the council never painted Marsha's
    place
I wondered if she drank and smoked heavily
Because she was alone
Waiting for someone to sweep her off her feet
I never did see any wedding photos when I used to visit

Back to the days when what you really wanted
Was to have a best friend
Someone you hoped would like you
Just for yourself
When intimacy was sharing the same bath
Or both of you having matching scarves
Like my friend Michael
Who passed away
Leaving me feeling like I would never smile again

Back to the days of the melodic sounds of Maureen
Calling her children in for tea
'John, Stephen, Rodney!'
To my favourite chocolate-coated sweets
They used to call treats
And when two half-pennies made one whole penny
And now my memories of those times
Are like describing a vivid dream
Now it is 1996
And I have been married two whole weeks.

PERFORMANCE POETRY AND THE SPOKEN WORD

POETRY AROUND THE CLOCK

To de top
To de top
To de top
My programme can't flop
Because me deh pan de poetry
Right around de clock...

Wid lyrics dat me fire
Like a rocket launcher
I don't come for breakfast
Lunch or tea
I come for dinner
So roast off de breadfruit
Fry off snappa
Show some respect
I am the storyteller

Wid de broom dat me sweep wid
Me no miss no corner
I got someting to say yes
To all sufferers
Me arm up meself
Me inna your corner
To fight fe truths and rights
Beat down all oppressors

Now plenty in de crew
But de more a we de better
Nah send dis by text
Nah send dis by letter
Me deh pan de stage

To put de whole ting propa
Suggesting dat we put
Put we brains dem togedda
Organise weself
An create a new structure
A ghetto education
Wid a whole heap of culture

To de top...

Wid lyrics dat me fire...

THE SPOKEN WORD

I have my foundation
It is here I make my stand
It is solid as a rock
It will not sink into the sand

For de rock where I stand pan
Is de spoken word tradition
An right now me a lift it
To its rightful position

Despite the opposition
Me have me ammunition
Me no want my people tink say
Dat me lost me education

For de spoken word was here
Before we wrote it down on paper
Respect to my ancestors
If I deny myself this truth
Then to myself I am a traitor

So big up
Big up
To the cultural orators
Like Marcus Garvey
Who made me proud of me colour

Rosa Parks & Dr. Martin Luther King Jr. in 1965

And Martin Luther King
Left us with words
That we could savour
A caged bird must be free
Respect to Paul Laurence Dunbar

And if you try to diss this style
I know I have the answer
I'll fall back on a proverb
If it means it makes you wiser
I have plenty of tricks
Just like Anansi the spider

So if you want to test me
I will trap you in your corner
Return you to your roots
Like Sojourner Truth.

POETRY REVIVAL

Wheel an come again my selector
Dis is revival time
Wheel an come again my supa
For poetry's running wild
Now dat a fe me writing style
Watch you now
Dat a fe me writing style

I want to relate
I need a bit a space
Poetry is the way
That I can define me place
In a de rat race

I say I need me space
For poetry is the way
Dat I can put a name
To my complaint

So if I want to give it a musical twist
Or drop it like a criss biscuit
That is my prerogative
For I am counteracting the rules
Of what I can and cannot do
It is an issue of which I have plenty of views
So for those of you who do not have a clue
I'm free to do
I'm free to choose

Wheel an come again my selector…

Now some say dat me wicked
An some say dat me wile
But what I really want is to be versatile
I want to tek it to black
I want to tek it to white
In truth I want to leave you
On a poetry high

So if I spy with my little eye
A poet that can spin me a lyrical line
That tells me that they've got their eyes on life
It's like being in a blues
Listening to a revival tune

So wheel an come again my selector…

YOUTH

NO WASH YOUR MOUTH OVER YOUTHS

It takes a community to raise our children
But the system don't understand
Dem say children have too much liberation
And no community to take dem in hand

Some say it is a change of circumstance
For you can't tell mumma from child
Both a dance pan de same dance floor
Wearing the same designer style

And the traditional cultural values
Dat was deh wid we from time
Well dem not instilling it again
No not inna dem family life

Some say it is because
There is no father in the home
That boys need a positive role model
To keep dem on the rightful road

While others say
Dat is just an excuse
The children of today are too blasted rude
Bring back de hanging
Bring back de birch
Tek dem off de streets
And mek dem go to church

While others say you see now
You see how the world now turn
I remember de good old days
When children were seen and never heard

You could beat dem
Yes beat dem
Dat is how dem would learn
A dem de kind of values
We should a tek time and preserve

But tell me Sista Murray
And a want you tell me true
You would like your children
Wash dem mouth so over you

And what are we as de adults
Going to roll up we sleeve and do
For de other day I was sitting down
Just sitting down watching de news

When a government minister
Come on de telly an say
He would like to hug a hoody
Till the eyes dem protrude

Well Sista Murray
A me ask you
Him really want to squeeze de bwoy
Till the eyes pop out for true?

If dat is de case
Then dis government minister is really very rude
And him same self
Don't have de right attitude

Sista Murray nod her head
And say all a dat is true
All a dat is true
An nuttin nah improve

Me answer her begrudgingly
Begrudgingly in truth
Yes Sista Murray
Dat sad
But true...

BIG UP DE YOUTHS

Big up de youths
Who a do dem very best
Big up de youths
Who nah run wid badness
Big up de youths
Who have dem eyes pan de prize
Big up de youths
Who a struggle but a try

To take care of environment
Look after de sick
Give time to their communities
Widout wages
Dem nah rob
And dem no tief
And dem no up to no tricks
Dem a look after dem body
Dem a run circuits
Dem a go to school and college
An a do dem learning
You no see de topper grades
That they're achieving

So big up de youths...

To deal with the stigma
Of being stereotyped
Taking adult orders
While they don't have no voice
But some a overcome it
An a mek de right choice
Dem a overcome de problem
Want their futures to be bright
It's time for we as adults now
To give de youths a bligh

So big up de youths...

BRAVADO

So you think you're in the in
You think you're in the know
But it's only half a story
Till the other side is told
Hear my flow
Melting ice-caps in the North Pole
Turning heads from here to Cairo
With prophecies revealed
Prophecies unfold
I'll tell you to your face
How you're losing control
Of mind, body and soul

Moving with your foes
Marking out your territory
Sniffing out your bones
You think you're going places
Yet you've got no place to go
Happy slapping clapping
And filming on your phone
You think you cracking jokes
But you and I know
That's just bravado
You and I know
That's just bravado

So you think you're in the in...

Responding cool to whore
Accepting that low status
And you call that street code
But we know who you are
Though you hide behind your shadows
You're a person with potential
Yet you're moving like you're shallow
Acting like you don't care
I don't buy that for a moment
Because you and I know
That's just bravado
You and I know
That's just bravado

That's just bravado
Your insecurities on show
So let us who believe in you
Help you reach your goals
You may be feeling let down
See my views as somewhat hollow
But while you're thinking that today
I think of your tomorrows.

THE YOUTHS A BEG FOR LIFE

Am coming with the grit of Bessie Smith
To say de youths a beg for life
Like Oliver Twist
And a spoonful of sugar
Cannot change the taste of this
When de youths dem pan de street say
Dat we are the hypocrites

Every day dat dey wake up
They got to face the culprits
Some a do dem lickle bess
But dem nah mek a profit
And the adults turn dem back
Because dem can't face it

What a diss
If we don't own up to it
What a diss
Dem nah go put up wid it

You know the cap fits
Yet you still won't wear it
The history of the youths man
You just got to hear it
There's no need to run
No need to fear it
Try to overstan how de youths
Might be feeling
Try to overstan how they
Might express it

Bessie Smith (1894-1937)

When they mark up on the walls
In order to be seen
Those who do not overstan
Sight graffiti
Yet there's another way
In which that could be seen
How de youths dem pan de streets
Now a face a tight squeeze

With the funding
And the funding
And the closing down
The funding
And the funding
So they're roaming around

So am coming with the grit of Bessie Smith...

Dem done see
How you done look after
Dis precious planet
And they know that some adults in a life
Cannot be trusted
You put de youths dem inna home
You find they are accosted

Education is the key
But the school is barely standing
Some using the rod now
To create overstanding
Don't want them to respond though
Don't want them to be angry
Don't want us to know
That the youths have some feelings

So am coming with the grit of Bessie Smith...

WHO A GO TELL DE YOUTHS DEM STORY

Who a go tell de youths dem story
Going overboard can't escape that it's gory
Worse than the horrors I does see in horror movies
Got to make a stand I'll be neglecting my duties

For no amount of blood and guts compares to the
    grooming
Youths upon youths now sexually abusing
Moving like wolves with their pack mind mentality
Cannot recognise now the blurring of the boundaries

Who a go tell de youths dem story...

For true say we have the gangster mentality
Youths are not free to move in their communities
Banned from certain areas and certain territories
Stripped of their childhoods before they're really ready
A move wid a crew dat say no study
Mek your money
No respect for self
No respect nobody
And getting use to stepping over younger dead bodies

Who a go tell de youths dem story...

So I will speak out about the wicked atrocities
Persistent cruelties
Gather up the names of the safeguarding agencies
I want de youths out there to know that they can trust me
Me no inna de blaming
But childhood's going down the drain
We need to be reclaiming
Naming the culprits
Rehabilitating
Pursuing on this course
Until it's from the same page we are reading

Who a go tell de youths dem story...

GET AN EDUCATION

Yes you love your life
Yes you love your life
So you nah go run with gang or gun
Or move with any knife

You a go cultivate your gifts
Like the bee in a de hive
Cultivate your talents
Want your honey to be nice

Because just like the bee
You're more central to my life
The bee pollinates the plants
So each one a we can strive
So get an education
Though the circumstance no nice
For once you have that education
You have it now for life

So yes you love your life...

But let me tell you plainly
What is really on the line
When you don't have education
No money put aside
You move wid bad company
A dem a run your life
Yes you a do de talking
But who a draw de line
The shine from de bling
Have cataracts pan your eyes

You only know you lost your freedom
When the guard say out the light
Incarcerated once
No incarcerated twice
Once in the mind
And now you doing time

So yes you love life...

RACISM AND SEXISM

REBELLIOUS ONE

I am Africa steeped in sun
I am where this story begun
I am known as the rebellious one
Working this land
And praying for freedom

I am the black woman who must walk upright
I am the one who must close my eyes to spite
For I know apartheid of any kind isn't right
So I march
I march with my brothers and sisters
To keep up the fight
It is only right

I am the black woman
Who reads those newspapers every day
I know there are people out there
That don't want things to change
But unity is strength
So gather all we are going to need
If we intend to live in one harmony

For I am Africa steeped in sun
I am where this story begun
I am known as the rebellious one
Working this land
And praying for freedom.

BNP EXPOSED

The BNP think they are indigenous
That is ridiculous
With the knowledge of my history
Going to dress you down meticulous
Indigenous that's so ridiculous
With the knowledge of my history
Going to dress you down meticulous
Dress you down meticulous

For Africa is all of us
I think about the Ice Age
And I can't take you so serious
No matter how you look at it
You really couldn't be first
Are you Anglo-Saxon, Celtic
Or just getting on my nerves

Indigenous that is ridiculous
And with the knowledge of my history
Going to dress you down meticulous
Indigenous that's so ridiculous
With the knowledge of my history
Going to dress you down meticulous

Nick Griffin is an immigrant
He really has no argument
Insisting on spreading all his venomous ignorance
On purity and race
Yet our race built up de place
And purity does not exist
So let's cut to the chase

Canute, King of England, Denmark and Norway

King Canute was from Denmark
William the Conqueror was French
Can't you see by those examples
The cultural influence
If you analyse it good Nick
Your words don't make no sense
And I can make the point now
By adding all the rest
James the First was from Scotland
William of Orange was Dutch
And George the First was German man
Case closed
Rapped up
And shut

Indigenous that is ridiculous
And with the knowledge of my history
I done dress you down meticulous
Indigenous that's so ridiculous
And with the knowledge of my history
I done dress you down meticulous
Indigenous ridiculous
For Africa is all of us.

SPIRITUALLY LIFTED

Spiritually lifted
Spiritually gifted
Ancestors stay alive
Through the words
That we're expressing
We ain't stressing
We're just assessing
The system with the message
That they left before the passing

So for those who might be interested
For those who might be asking
Yes we're counteracting
We're beating round no bush
I'll say you're blatantly lying
When you said we came with nothing
But ourselves when we had landed

Yet Tate and Lyle still striving
From the cane that we were cutting
That needed the strength
And the spirit sustaining
With long time sayings
That were stored in the memory
Culture retained through the re-telling of stories
Oppression released
Through traditional dances
A reconstruction of oneself
In a strange man's country
A phenomenal achievement
Swept under the carpet

Cutting the sugar cane

Yet many of us have survived this journey
Spiritually lifted
Spiritually gifted
Ancestors stay alive
Through the words
That we're expressing
And we ain't stressing
We're just assessing
The system with the message
That they left before the passing.

STEREOTYPE

If you want to get to know me
To see me more deeply
Don't try to know me
By the clothes that I'm wearing
Because anyone who knows me
Knows that words should have meaning
And I will take you on
If I think you're stereotyping

If you want to get to know me
To see me more deeply
Don't try to know me
By the way that I'm walking
I am a stickler for justice
I will walk miles to get it
Even though some say
That it's non-existent

If you want to get to know me
To see me more deeply
Then get a little insight
From the questions you ask me
Don't assume or act
Like you already know me
Or share the stereotypical views
That you're getting from the telly

If you want to get to know me
To see me more deeply
Don't try to find a box
In which you can put me

I don't like the feeling
Of being claustrophobic
Only caught in a tight space
Not kicking
But screaming
That's right.

MIXTURES IN THE RACE

Some say dem racist a lot
Some say dem racist a bit
An some say dem believe in live an let live
Some say Enoch Powell was right
Britain getting less white
An some say racism is a ting dem tired fight

Some a put we to de test
Some a mek dem progress
Some a mek de spirit dormant
Some a mek it restless
Some a see it an a talk it
Some a see it couldn't care less
An some say dat de wickedness has firmly manifest

Now some a celebrate
The mixtures in the race
An some still bex an full up a hate
Some a come togedda
An some a separate
An some still believe
Dat you better know your place
In the race
People battle on regardless in the race
Some loss dem life pan de way
But some live to fight another day
Many victories have been won this way.

THE BRAIN IS THE BLING

I used to put it on
A looks me a go live on
Put it on a dat me a depend pon
Put it on a looks me a go live on
But wha me a go do
When me good looks gone

Me going wish me did get
A little education
Instead a see me self
Through de eyes of a man
Dat deh noose been round
My neck for far too long
Nuttin nah gwan
Unless me have a man
Me never hear bout the word
Dey call it independence
No de rent gotta pay
So de wax gone on

Me say put it on
A looks me a go live on
Put it on a dat me a depend pon
Put it on a looks me a go live on
But wah me a go do
When me good looks gone

Me going wish me did leggo
Mama apron string
Embrace all de good
An dash way negative ting
Stop see de body shape
As de place where me think
I would a tek out me brain
Out a de bargain bin
Darn it on yes like Gucci an ting
And mek de man know
Dat the brain is the bling

Instead a put it on
A looks me a go live on
Put it on a dat me a depend pon
Put it on a looks me a go live on
But wha me a go do
When me good looks gone.

GET UP STAND UP

Get up stand up
For a your time now woman
Let the breeze touch your face
Let the world embrace you woman

You never let the wind blow you down
You never let the rain make you drown
Experience is a thing
Why you will always be around now woman

Look how long you have been steering that ship
You make it look like there is nothing to it
But only you can give it credit now woman

Bob Marley (1945-1981)

Benjamin Zephaniah

So come out a de winter
An enter into spring
Coz that is the time
When nature's nurturing
No badda mek de wickedness
Get into your runnings now woman

Always look forward
Never look back
Know that from time
That you've been held back
But what's in the heart
Can't be bought with cash
So put away the stash
You don't need to prove
Yourself to any man

Just get up stand up
For a your time now woman
Let the breeze touch your face
Let the world embrace you woman.

RAISE UP THE LOW

Raise up the low
Bring down the mighty
That's what we do
To bring about equality
We line up we self
With all man like Shelley
For they are few
And we are many

Many a work
And see none a de money
Children work in sweat shops
Yet dem walk de streets scruffy
You want the work do
No want to see your hands dirty
Toilet cleaning
Sweeping streets
You find dat too lowly
Employ de immigrants
And pay dem lousy
When you look now
You done turn dem into enemy
Racists a say
Dem taking over de country
We know they're making you
A whole heap a money

Me say raise up the low...

Protest meeting in Trafalgar Square, London, 1959

Remember when dem use to
Say de same ting to we
Are you a monkey?
Do you swing from trees?
No blacks
No dogs
No Irish
If you please
And what you doing here?
Go back to your country
Me say sambo and nigga
Was a few names for we
You rarely saw a black face on the TV
You were taking a risk

When you went out a street boy
Beaten by the public
Beaten by police
They would say you was dunce
An you really can't read
At de bottom of the barrel
Is where dem had we

Now you're sat in a Babylon
Wid flat screen TV
A run off your mouth
With selective memory
It's a lack of education
If you know what a mean
If you can't show the immigrant
No sympathy
If you can't align yourself
With a shared story
Then you're doing to the immigrants
What Britain did to we

So raise up the low...

NATURE

RESPECT MUDDA NATURE

You tink mudda nature easy
Mudda nature not easy at all
Mudda nature come in like
The pride you know
Like the pride before the fall

Mudda nature has within her
The wind, the sun and the rain
Mudda nature commands the skies
The seas and all of land terrain

And although mudda nature
Is often ignored
She raise up sugar cane
She raise up corn
She has been looking after her children
From the time dem born
Not always getting her just rewards

And so the children grow
But they don't listen when she talks
They don't want to remember
When she was the calm after the storm

So they go about their business
Treating the planet as they like
Not giving mudda nature a second thought
Not following her advice

And now the ice-caps dem are melting
And plenty countries are facing drought

And many people are wondering
What's the weather all about

Animals face extinction
Through the changing habitat
You tink mudda nature
Sitting back and liking all a dat
No!

But true say mudda nature love we
And true say mudda nature smart
Mudda nature nah go tek we now
And slap we hard, hard, pan we arse

Instead she is going to give us the guidance
On how to preserve this planet
Before it lost
But this time all her children will learn
Just how much this costs.

A MOMENT'S THOUGHT IN SOUTHWOLD

Today I saw the sky touching the sea
Well that is how it appeared to me
A simple illustration in shades of opal blue emerald
    green
That things are not always as they seem
As I sat in Southwold
Watching the sky touching the sea.

Rosa on a Suffolk beach

THE VIEW OUTSIDE MY WINDOW

I hope I never take for granted
The view outside my window
Especially the one I am looking at now
The sun is teasing the leaves
Of the tall silver birch at the end of the garden
Bringing about a light that exposes the many shades of
    green
From time to time a breeze would cause those leaves to
    sway delicately

**Silver birch in
our garden**

On the window-sill the determined geraniums
Are leaning over to the right
Still strong though not upright
Both the gate and the sky
With the help of the surrounding rose bushes
And evergreen leaves
Seem to be protecting us
My daughter and I
From the world outside
For as long as we desire

It is October
And soon those leaves will fall
And then there'll be another view
Which I hope will stay in my memory.

FLOWERS

The sweet smell of summer jasmine
Can perfume the evening air
And fuchsias can hang like lanterns
As if designed to be leading the way
Laburnum can drop like well-nurtured dreadlocks
The foxglove wears the blouse of a sexy lady
And once the rose has a rose
Watch her strike a pose – vogue
The red-hot pokers stand to attention
Overlooking the buttercup carpet
And the seeded dandelions floating around
Remind me of Shakespearian fairies
The star-shaped periwinkles in the garden
Sway like a traditional gospel choir
And the little forget-me-nots they sit in the corner
While listening intently to their elders.

ANCESTORS' TIME ON HAMPSTEAD HEATH

Come, come celebrate with me
For it is ancestors' time on Hampstead Heath
You will see it in the red gold and green
Of weeping willow
Great oak
And sycamore tree
You will see the colours
Of the Ethiopian flag
That means so much
To many a we

You will see joyful children
Playing with ancestors
Represented in the various browns
Of the crisping leaves
They may not know that those colours
Represent the colours of my people
That made that treacherous journey
Across the sea
Bringing about a richness
Of colour, culture
That is now in so many of our communities

So come, come and celebrate with me
For it is ancestors' time on Hampstead Heath
You will see it
In the red gold and green
Of weeping willow
Great oak
And sycamore tree

And if you look behind
One of those great big trees
Who knows
You may see me!

HISTORY AND POLITICS

TALKING BOOK

Reading a book is a political act
I wish someone had've taught me that
I wish I had've known of the sacrifices made
So that I could simply sit, turn the page

It is only now that I am mature in age
I look back on those mundane days
Sitting in classrooms bored out of my brains
I'm listening to the teachers express in such an
    unexpressive way
The tiny words written on that academic page
That if understood will get me a job some day

Some day I won't need this place
Reading will take second place
I don't need words to conquer me
I will learn all I need from the streets
Till the streets taught me
That nothing in life is free
That every freedom that I have
Has been earnt politically

Even the freedom of being able to read
Someone fought for that for me
So let us come together
Let us check out this history
For the reality me a deal with
Is slavery

Asher and Rosa in Gorée Island, Dakar, Senegal

Now William Wells Brown
He knows what I mean
He wanted to read so bad
He couldn't even sleep
He used to bribe the white street children
With a lick of his sweet
Because he knew being able to read
Would mean power, don't you see

See-saw, Marjorie Daw
Check out this man
Them call him Gronniosaw

Now he, my friends
Was an African prince
Captured as a slave
Sailed on the slave ship
Observed his master reading to his crew
Decided he would like to do that too

William Wells Brown
(1814-1884)

But when he raised the book up to his ear
It never made a sound
So he went in search to find out
Where that secret could be found

What was the difference
Between the master and he
Why did words not jump out and speak
Maybe those words
Maybe they despise me

Can't you see how that's important
Can't you see how that is deep
I don't need no more than that
To try and convince me

That reading a book is a political act
I wish someone had've taught me that
I wish I had've known of the sacrifices made
So that I could simply sit and turn the page.

AHEAD OF YOUR TIME

To be ahead of your time
Could mean that you are marginalized
Because no one likes the idea
That they might be left behind
It's as if they are saying
What right do you have
To open my eyes
Before their time
If I can't see it
It must be a lie
To really appreciate what I say
Let's look at the life of William Blake
He was described as a lunatic
Make no mistake
But now he takes his place in history
He is admired and revered
So many years later
Now he has no ears to hear.

William Blake (1757-1827)

BIDE YOUR TIME

Bide your time
Is a saying worth remembering
It conjures up the feeling that patience is rewarded
Today it was announced that Mandela is coming
And the city of London is now preparing

He will be welcomed by his enemies
He will be welcomed by friends
He will be welcomed by those
Who thought apartheid wouldn't end
He'll be welcomed by those who thought
He was a terrorist
He'll be welcomed by those who believe
In justice

Bide your time
Now that's a saying worth remembering
For it conjures up the feeling that patience is rewarded
Today it was announced that Mandela is arriving

He could have taken his revenge
When he visited the queen
She never did support him
In the apartheid regime

He could have taken his revenge
With the hyper journalists
But with a smile and a step
He showed us what it's like to have real respect

Slogan in Forest Gate, London E 7

Bide your time
Is a saying worth remembering
For it conjures up the feeling that patience is rewarded
And this was demonstrated the day Mandela came to
    Brixton
And the people lined the streets
For those were the people he wanted to meet
They stood by him through thick and thin
When all the odds were stacked against him
For don't the Brixton people in more ways than one
Share the experience of this great man
GUILTY WITHOUT FAIR TRIAL!
In a Babylon jail nuff a dem die
But some nah waste dem time
Pouring water from dem eye
Dem a spen dem whole life
Just a stand up for dem rights

Bide your time
It's a saying worth remembering
For it conjures up the feeling that patience is rewarded
And this was demonstrated
The day apartheid was defeated.

SO YOU NEVER VOTE!

Sound bites
Bite the dust
Protect those
Who are corrupt
Slipping down
The slippery slope
Politics becomes a joke

The people say
They have no hope
Without the hope
There is no vote
Without the vote
Without the hope
There is no hope for change

Rise up mighty people
Stand up for your rights
Stop taking things for granted
Taking history for a ride

Remember where you come from
And all what's yet to come
We still a chant down Babylon
Plenty more to be done

Don't sit down on the sofa
As if your bottom's stuck
Now we have man like Boris Johnson
Ruling over us

PRESIDENT NELSON MANDELA AND THE PEOPLE OF SOUTH AFRICA

Let that be a lesson
Never to forget
The vote was born from sacrifice
It is us the vote protects

Unless you get complacent
Unless you do forget
The sacrifice of Mandela
And the suffragettes.

DON'T ATTACK IRAQ

Dem mek dem pack
To attack Iraq
But we a counteract
Because we nah go tek dat

Bush and Blair behaving
Like gutter rats
So now we got de gutter rats
We gotta set a trap

Buss dem in dem head
Like David wid a sling shot
Buss dem in dem head
But Lord
Buss dem wid the facts
For to tek a youth life
Man a wickedness dat
Who is responsible for that?

Who will take the blame
Who will take the shame
You can't take another man's life
And do it in my name

So that is why we a campaign
We nah sit pan we arse
An a drink champagne
We a write we letters
We a write dem wid complaints
We a post dem to de House of Parliament
Right away

Martin and Rosa against the war in Iraq

Coz we want a serious word wid Mr Blair
We want to know
We want to know
Why he can't feel despair

Now dem mek dem pack to attack Iraq
Like we no know wha dem a do behind we back
Selling arms to Iraq
Kick back an relax
A wha you call dat?
A hypocrite dat
But we done see through dat
Hear de gun dem a pop
An while you sleep in a you bed
Others live in dread
While you sleep in a you bed
Others live in dread

Your conscience that must be dead
The life that you're living well that is ill-spent
A life for a life could never make no sense
You hide behind a regime
But the oil is your intent
That's what makes you content
It makes you just like Saddam himself

Now you mek you pack
To attack Iraq
But we a counteract
Ca we nah go tek dat
Bush and Blair behaving
Like gutter rat
But now we have de gutter rat
We going to set a trap

Buss dem in dem head
Like David wid a sling shot
Buss dem in dem head
But Lord…
Buss dem wid de facts
For to tek a youth life
Man a wickedness dat
Who is responsible for that?

Who will take the blame
Who will take the shame
You can't take another man's life
And do it in my name.

BRAVE SOLDIERS

Brave soldiers in Afghanistan
Worried families wait at home
Take some comfort in the thought
That their loved ones are hailed as heroes
Heroes who have courage
Heroes who are bold
Those sentiments are warm
As bodies come home cold

Raised high upon the concourse
Wrapped in red, white and blue
A routine announcement heard
On the radio and on the news
I immediately think of the families
The life-time pain they will have to bear
The sorries from the dignitaries
Whose children won't die there

Brave soldiers in Afghanistan...

So my thoughts are often troubled
I don't want to show no disrespect
But are the government cutting budgets
While our soldiers risk their necks?
Too many civilians now have died
No end seems to be in sight
Just more suicide bombers
Improvised explosive device
More destruction more debris
This is no way of life

Brave soldiers in Afghanistan...

So after years of war-torn tragedies
Is it wrong to want some peace?
Now we're hearing of ex-soldiers
Living rough-shod on our streets
For some are not so lucky
Can't get prosthetic limbs
Others cannot find a job
We don't value their skills
Some turn to drugs
Others turn to drink
Others find their own ways and means
And end up in the clink

Brave soldiers in Afghanistan...

A NATION OF BANKERS

Once a nation of shopkeepers
Now we're a nation of banks
The rich are in the shit
So the poor must bail you out
Of a system we knew had to
Go into melt-down
Economically flat
No value to the pound
People losing jobs
Places closing down
Big pensions for the fat cats
While we live hand to mouth

No money tucked away in no Swiss bank account
No fat cheque for running the trains into the ground
No fast track for me into the teaching profession
You see the poor do the dole
The poor do repossessions

There is no accounting
For government solutions
That keeps us in the red
In a life-time of debt
For our children into adulthood
To live to regret
Because decisions made on their behalf
Not in their interest

Once a nation of shopkeepers...

COALITION

We get a coalition coalition
Because the people dem
Can't trust their politicians
Look how long dem making
Detrimental decisions
A hide behind power and position

Now dem a struggle now
To find a solution
Yet dem a run de programme
Rugged from creation
For years de pressure
Bearing down on the nation
With the rocketing of exploitation
The spending on the wars
And not to mention
De work and sweat
And broke your neck
No mek no money yet
The state of the economy
A noose around your neck
To get a education
Garn deep in a de debt
The rise in petty crime
Well dem nah study the effects
It's the rich that they protect

So we get a coalition coalition...

While the gap between the rich and poor gets wider
Dem a draw back pan de money mek you poorer
Say we got to tighten up we belt for de future
But some have it so tight dem a keel over
A look for what fe borrow
A look for what fe pawn
Years of paying a mortgage
Now you don't have no yard
De little strength what dem have now
Is de faith dem have in God

So me no want to hear bout consequence
Me no want to hear bout cause
When you know dat disya system
Could a get dis ting resolve
The riots of the 80's
Is not nothing to ignore
If you open up Pandora's box
Then what you have is war!

So we get a coalition coalition...

While de gap between the rich and poor gets wider
Dem a draw back pan de money mek you poorer
Say we got to tighten up we belt for de future
But some have it so tight dem a keel over!

WE LIVING TOO LONG!

The government has brought it to our attention
Dat we got to put more money in a we pension
So de people dem a question
How the government draw dat conclusion

For when we working too long
We want kick back and relax
But you living too long
Dem can mek a money out a dat
So they're rooting for the people
To work until dem drop
And wid de money dat dem save
They can bridge de debt gap

Rosa on the march

Dat is legitimizing tiefing
The people won't accept dat
You gwine see how de people feel
When everyting stop
No bus, no train, no school, no shop
People need de money
But everyting stop
For we a run de programme
Dem done forget dat
Catch we left, right and centre
Wid pay freeze and VAT

So a beg you wid we pension
Keep your dirty hands of a dat
For we nah bruck back
To pay off the banks
No thanks
No thanks
No thanks
No thanks!

DANCE IN YOUR YARD

Dance in your yard
Before you dance abroad
Ca you nah go look so good
If people tink say you a fraud

Defend your little corner
But be deh pan you guard
You need the strength
Of the Almighty to step on the path

Can't always practise what we preach
Because we know dat life hard
But if you do your little best
The Father gives you de applause

Me nah forward
Nah rewind
Me no deh pan no pause
When you see me in a action bwoy
You know me have a cause
Me no speaky-spokey
Pretty pretty
Build up no rapport
Me a shack out
An a broke out
An a come a little more
About de guns and de tanks
Keeping de people dem poor
Civilians dead a ground
A beg you look a little more

See your sons and your daughters
Then don't do that no more
For prevention for real
Must be better than the cure

So done with the talking
We done hear dat before
Leggo de wickedness
De wickedness of war

Wid de money dat you save
You could a do plenty more
To build up opportunities
And open plenty doors

And those who are naked
Mek sure we sort out some clothes
And those who are thirsty
Mek de good water flow

Put de roof pan de school
Fix the holes in a de road
A home is not a luxury
I want you to know
We just asking for the things
That you would want for your own

So dance in your yard...

Me say dance in a your yard
Before you dance abroad
Abroad
Abroad
Before you dance abroad.

PUT UP A FIGHT

Some people a complain
Dem no like de way de work-place
A shape up nowadays
Some say the minute
Dem turn dem back
More of the workers gettin de sack
Those who lef back nah talk back
Not while dem a hole
A temporary contract

Everybody a try deal wid de situation
In dem own way
Some dey off sick
Some a discuss it
Some garn independent
Some garn co-operative
And some pray to God
Dem could win de lottery

But the general consensus
Seems to be that the management
Is not treating the workers properly
This is something that has been
Going on throughout history
It's a real tragedy when people
Get their kicks out of other people's misery

No tink say Thatcher did not know
What she was doing
When she bring in she legislation
To try dismantle de union

Got de management
A joy-ride wid people life
A sack and a hire
An a do as dem like

But all good tings for dem
Must come to an end
For history dictates that again and again
So while we're on the subject
Let us mek a list
To remind de management
Dat dem jus can't win

The Peasants' Revolt nearly brought down de king
Harriet Tubman set slaves free
Sojourner Truth stood up for her rights
Rosa Parks brought about Civil Rights

Harriet Tubman
(c.1820-1913)

Sojourner Truth
(c.1797-1883)

The Miners' Strike 1984-85

You don't remember the Miners' Strike
Now all those people had one thing in common
They were seen as a people without no powers
So let that be your inspiration
Let that be your guide
You don't need fists
To put up a fight.

AN EYE FOR AN EYE

An eye for an eye, a tooth for a tooth
How long have we been juggling this view we say is truth
Yet an eye for an eye and everybody would be blind
These are the words of Gandhi
Still touching hearts and minds
A man of passive resistance, humility and pride
Essential tools I believe if we are to navigate through life
But Gandhi is not the only knight that sits about my table
Keeping me able keeping me stable
Because it isn't always easy to be so honourable
In a system that can make you feel
As if circumstances are insurmountable
Yet still we rise
We rise because Maya Angelou was wise
So she too enters the room with those good knights
To share her good advice

Claudia Jones (1915-1964)

Louise Bennett
(1919-2006)

But not before she's rushed over to Martin Luther King
She observes James Baldwin from ear to ear grinning
She takes a loving look at her sister Claudia Jones
Louise Bennett gives her that Jamaican welcome home
Mandela jumps up to organise her seat
Slovo announces it's time for us to eat
Yes these are the knights that sit about my table
Keeping me able keeping me stable
Because it isn't always easy to be so honourable
In a system that can make you feel
As if circumstances are insurmountable
But with the advice from my good knights
I rise
I rise
I rise
There I go.

HAPPINESS

LA PALMA IS...

La Palma is shimmering sun shining
Through the gaps of the leaves of the banana trees

La Palma is home-rolled cigars
Neatly sown embroidery

La Palma is hard-working fishermen
Beside the sea

La Palma is freshly caught fish
For my husband, daughter and me

La Palma is recently washed clothes
Put out to dry

La Palma is coffee drunk on hill-top side
Freshly cooked meals you could eat outside

La Palma is friendly people
With lovely sunny smiles

La Palma is pineapple, water melon
Swimming in the sea

La Palma is the place
To inspire a poet like me.

Asher & Rosa in La Palma

THE VERSATILE SMILE

A smile to me is a survival technique
It has within it all my beliefs
For a smile can tell many a story

A smile can say you have had a past
And now appreciate your present

A smile can say
You would rather have friends
Than a whole load of enemies

A smile can say
Have faith
Good will to all men
And women

A smile can say
Count to ten
Please don't lose your rag again

A smile can say
I'm not fazed
You can't get inside my brain

A smile can say
I am sturdy
If you're so powerful
Take it from me.

WALK WITH...

Walk with confidence
Walk with pride
Walk with love
Walk with a smile
Walk with curiosity
Walk with sincerity
Walk like you know
Life's full of possibilities

Walk like you know
You got peace in mind
Walk like you know
You don't want to fight
Walk like you know
Your brain and your mouth
Is your most precious weapon
Walk like you know
Some will ask for your opinion

Respond with confidence
Respond with pride
Respond with love
Respond with a smile
Respond with curiosity
Respond with sincerity
And let other walkers know
Life's full
Life's full of possibilities.

CELEBRATING WOMEN'S VOICES

Being a woman
Can be so liberating
But sometimes we need
A little convincing
A touch of persuading
So I am listening to Aretha Franklin
Now she sings about the word Respect
Something women have fought
Hard to get

And I should know
Because I have been following the story of Nina Simone
And I know she hasn't received
Half the money for the records she sold
But just like Aretha she's got soul

Aretha Franklin

Joan Armatrading

And yes I've had my moans
But when I hear my sisters sing
I know we women can do our own thing

Because being a woman
Can be so liberating
But sometimes we need
A little convincing
A touch of persuading
So I am chilling with Joan Armatrading

Reflecting on the woman who had no voice
The woman who had no choice
The woman who's on the arm of this man
Who only wants her to exploit
And I'm longing to touch
The dry lands of my own shores

So let me pause
So that I can tell
That his reign does end

I began by opening my mouth
As wide as Patti Labelle
I shook my hips
Like Gladys Knight and the Pips
And simply said
I have had enough of this shit

What a liberating feeling that is
To be one of those liberated women.

THERE'S A PLACE FOR...

There's a place for love
There's a place for peace
There's a place for joy
There's a place for release

There's a place for war
There's a place for the poor
There's a place for those
Who always want more

There's a place for those
Who are looking for answers
There's a place for those
Who trod for justice
Not waiting for the hereafter
There's a place for those
Who write on placards rebellious and bold
That has brought so many in from out of the cold

There's a place I'm afraid
For more of the same
There's a place for those
Who have no shame
There's a place for those
Who have ears to hear
Eyes to see but will not open up
Will not come clean

There's a place for those
Who know that time is of the essence
There's a place for those who are insistent
There's a place for those who are persistent
And there's a place for those who put up resistance.

BRING THE DYSLEXIC BACK ON

I'd like to say you look exotic
But I'll probably say you look erotic
I'd like to say you're situated
But I may say you're saturated

Exotic
Erotic
Situated
Saturated

I want to call the whole thing
Should I call the whole thing
I want to call the whole thing off

Coz you'll see pursued
And I'll say persuaded
I'll read maintained
While you'll say it's marinated
Because maintained and marinated
Well that would change the meaning

I want to call the whole thing
Should I call the whole thing
Want to call the whole thing off

But oh….
If only I knew my phonics
I'd have a tactic
And oh if only I could really grasp it
Man I would practise…

Camels are mainly found in the dessert.

Ah, buh, cuh, duh, eh, fuh
Guh, huh, ih, juh, kuh, luh
Muh, nuh, oh, puh, quh, ruh
Suh, tuh, uh, vuh, wuh
X, yuh
X, yuh
Z
Z
Z
Z
Z

Then I wouldn't say you're eccentric
When I really mean you're electric
And I wouldn't say you've been relegated
When I mean I'm just regulating

Because I got myself some phonics
Found myself a tactic
Witness how I practise
So bring the dyslexic back on

abcdef (recited phonetically as above)
ghijkl
mnopqr
stuvw
xy
xy
z
z
z
z
z.....